HOW TO COOK LIKE MOM

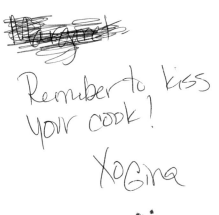

Remember to kiss
your cook!
XoGina

THE COOKBOOK
BY GINA SIMMONDS

ALL (AMATUER) PHOTOGRAPHY CREATED BY: GINA SIMMONDS
LAYOUT & EDITS BY: JAMES MURDOCK, TRUSTINJAMES CS AGENCY

GINASIMMONDS.COM

© 2022 Third Press

A LETTER TO MY BOYS

The three greatest things I have done in my life are marrying dad, having you two boys, and finally creating the best chicken pot pie! I love to cook and I want to pass on my passion for that art to you both. I want to send you both out into the world with the skills of knowing how to fend for yourself when it's time to eat, how to cook well, and to be confident in the kitchen and be able to cook for others.

So, I have made this cookbook easy to read and follow, with each recipe offering lots of tips and ideas. First mom tip, "Read through the whole recipe before you start!" You've seen me cook over the years and know I really don't use exact measurements and my goal is for you to do the same. Recipes are more like basic guidelines and you can tailor them to whatever you prefer, and whatever ingredients you have in your kitchen. Start out by using what I listed, tasting it along the way, and if you feel it needs a few sprinkles of something more, add it in. Just try not to go nutty on the salt at the beginning of a recipe. Start with the minimum and slowly add along the way.

Pretty soon you'll be comfortable with knowing which spices you like, and you'll be able to eyeball how much to use in a recipe. These recipes all call for the minimum amount of ingredients, but if you want to use fresh minced garlic instead of (for instance) garlic powder, go for it. Same goes for fresh herbs. In fact, it's a great idea to grow a little herb garden in a pot and use them in your recipes and of course, using different meats, veggies, or cheeses for recipes. It is all ok! Be creative!

I really want you two to think of the kitchen as the heartbeat of your home. Have fun, make memories, and learn how to create great food. None of this happens without some fails along the way. Make sure to write those down along with any notes in this cookbook for the next time you make the recipe. Oh, and don't forget to wash your dishes!!

DEDICATION

I WANT TO DEDICATE THIS BOOK TO MY HUSBAND PAUL, WHO IS ALWAYS MY #1 FAN. THANK YOU FOR THE MOTIVATION AND ALWAYS BELIEVING IN ME.
—P.S. I LOVE YOU!

STARTING OUT.

I've created a list of what you need to have a functional kitchen.

But, if you think of something else, write it down and get it when you can. Buying a basic utensil "set" is a great idea to start out.

Same goes with spices: Start with some basics, then as a recipe calls for it, buy the spice at that point. You can buy a small jar to start out with to see if you even like it. Stores are tricky with pricing- some smaller items are actually more expensive than the larger size so you need to have your head on the swivel!

And speaking of being alert while shopping, ALWAYS go grocery shopping with a list of at least your general idea of meals you plan to make. Mom Guaranteed, you'll always end up spending way more money than you planned if you don't have a list. Just think of all the junk food you have thrown into our cart when we have been grocery shopping together while I wasn't paying attention and ask yourself, "Do I actually want to pay for ALL THAT stuff myself this time??"

There' are a few basics that you really should have in your kitchen, pantry and refrigerator.

MOM TIP 101:

You'll always end up spending way more money than you planned if you don't go to the grocery store prepared with a plan. Ask yourself, "Do I actually want to pay for ALL THAT stuff myself??"

KITCHEN TOOL BASICS:

- Mixing Bowl set
- Wet Ingredients Measuring Cups
- Dry Ingredients Measuring Cups
- Spoon Measuring set
- Rubber Spatula (for mixing)
- Plastic Spatula (for a pan)
- Ladle, Large Spoon, slotted spoon set
- Frying Pan Set
- Pot Set
- Strainer
- Whisk
-
-

- Can Opener
- Peeler
- Ice Cream Scoop
- Wine & Beer Opener
- Grater
- Rimmed Cookie Sheets
- Electic Hand Mixer
- 12 Cupcake Baking Tin
- 9x13 Casserole Dish
- Set of Knives
- Cutting Boards
-
-

EXTRA TIPS

STOCKING BASICS.

DRY PANTRY GOODS:

- Kosher Salt
- Pepper
- Dried Thyme
- Dried Oregano
- Dried Basil
- Garlic Powder
- Onion Powder
- Chicken Bouillon
- Beef Bouillon
- Olive Oil
- Vegetable Oil
- Cooking Spray
- Red Wine Vinegar
- Soy Sauce (or Tamari)
- Hot Sauce
- Peanut Butter
- Jelly
-
-

- Hot Cocoa
- Coffee
- Rice
- Dijon Mustard
- Mayonnaise
- Catsup
- Canned Tuna
- Canned Beans
- Dry Pasta
- Canned Tomatoes
- Cereal
- Brown Sugar
- Sugar
- Vanilla Extract
- Baking Powder
- Baking Soda
- Flour (of your choice)
-
-

FRIDGE/FREEZER BASICS:

- Milk
- Eggs
- Bacon
- Onions
- Celery
- Carrots
- Salsa
- Cheese

- Bread (of your choice)
- Tortillas (of your choice)
- Frozen Peas
- Frozen Corn
- Sleeve of Hamburger Patties
-
-
-

PANTRY ITEMS

WELCOME HOME. LET'S START COOKING...

COOK LIKE MOM

RECIPES

MAINS 50

SNACKS & SAUCES 100

DESSERTS 110

BREAKFAST

1 PERSON   **TOASTER**   **5 MINUTES**   **$**

AVOCADO
TOAST

MOM TIP:

Another nice option would be to top with scrambled egg, cooked bacon or sliced tomato.

INGREDIENTS

2 Pieces of Bread

1 Avocado

Salt and Pepper to taste

pinch of chili flakes

DIRECTIONS

STEP 1

Toast 2 pieces of bread. While they are toasting, cut an avocado and slice or mash. Top the toast with avocado, salt, pepper, and chili flakes. Add any desired toppings.

CHILAQUILES
FROM MEXICO

BREAKFAST OF CHAMPIONS

This is definitely a house favorite :) You can use ham, shredded pork, leftover steak, shredded beef, anything for this recipe! I've also made these without meat and it was just as good.

2 PERSON   STOVETOP   15 MINUTES $

DIRECTIONS

STEP 1

In a large skillet over medium heat, add beef and salsa and saute for a couple minutes. Add eggs to the pan and scramble with the meat. As soon as the eggs begin to set, crush tortillas over the eggs (leave some big pieces) and stir into eggs while continuing to cook. Sprinkle cheese over.

STEP 2

Finish cooking until your eggs are the way you like them and serve. (I like to flip the eggs while the cheese is still sitting on top so the cheese goes to the bottom and gets a little crispy in the pan).

INGREDIENTS

1 Tablespoon Butter

1 Cup Beef, diced or shredded

3 Tablespoons Salsa

3 Eggs

2 Cups Tortilla Chips

½ Cup Cheese, shredded

Salt and Pepper to taste

CHRISTMAS BREAKFAST CASSEROLE

SUPEREASY

MOM TIP:

We have this every Christmas morning. If you have friends over for breakfast or you're going to a potluck brunch, make this. It's a winner! I always prepare this the night before and then in the morning I just pull it out from the fridge and bake it.

10 PERSON   **OVEN**   **50 MINUTES**   **$$**

INGREDIENTS

10 Eggs

½ cup Flour

1 teaspoon Baking Powder

1 pint Small Curd Cottage Cheese

1 pound Jack Cheese, grated

½ cup Butter, melted

8 ozs Diced Green Chilies

Salsa to serve on side

DIRECTIONS

STEP 1

Beat eggs in a large bowl. Add flour, baking powder, salt, cottage cheese, jack cheese, and melted butter. Mix until blended. Add green chilies and mix. Pour into a greased 9x13 pan. Bake at 350° for about 35—45 minutes or until the top is slightly browned.

STEP 2

Let stand a few minutes before serving. Serve with salsa on the side.

BREAKFAST

CINNAMON ROLLS
MASTERED.

MOM TIP

Store bought dough makes these treats quick and easy to make. Pictured is Gluten Free frozen Pizza dough, and they were fantastic! Make sure your dough is thawed completely for easy rolling.

MAKES 12 PCS   OVEN   35 MINS $

INGREDIENTS

1 loaf of Frozen Bread Dough or
1 Frozen Pizza Dough, thawed.

2 Tablespoons Butter, melted

3 Tablespoons Brown Sugar

1 Tablespoon Cinnamon

½ cup Powdered Sugar

1 teaspoon Vanilla Extract

2—4 Tablespoons Milk

DIRECTIONS

STEP 1

Roll thawed dough on a lightly floured board to a rectangle about 11x14 inches. Spread butter on dough to about an inch of each edge of dough. Sprinkle brown sugar over butter followed by cinnamon.

STEP 2

Roll up lengthwise and cut into 1 ½" circles. Place the rolls in a shallow baking dish about ½" to each other. Let sit to rest for about 25 minutes. Then bake at 350° for about 20—25 minutes or until dough is baked.

STEP 3

Let cool. In a small bowl, mix the powdered sugar, milk and vanilla to your liking for icing. Frost over cinnamon rolls.

CINNAMON TOAST
QUICK & EASY

This has been Dad's favorite to make for you boys because it was his favorite thing to eat, growing up.

1 PERSON **TOASTER** **5 MINUTES** **$**

INGREDIENTS

2 Pieces of Bread

¼ cup Powdered Sugar

¼ cup Brown Sugar

¼ cup White Granulated Sugar

1 teaspoon Cinnamon

Butter

DIRECTIONS

STEP 1

Begin toasting the pieces of bread. In a baggie or a bowl, begin mixing sugars, powdered sugar and cinnamon.

STEP 2

Butter both sides of the toast and place in a large baggie, one at a time. Shake to coat.

DENVER STRATA

ALL DAY BREAKFAST

MOM TIP:

You can play around with this recipe by changing the type of cheese, bread, seasonings or types of ham. Use what you have in your fridge. This is a great recipe to use leftover baguette from the night before as well!

 4 PERSON
 OVEN
 25 MINUTES
 $

DIRECTIONS

INGREDIENTS

1 Baguette, sliced about ½ inch thick

12 slices of Deli Ham

1 ½ cups Cheddar Cheese, shredded

6 Eggs

1 ½ cups Milk

2 Tablespoons Chopped Green Chilies

½ teaspoon Dried Thyme

2 Tablespoons Chopped Cilantro

3 Green Onions, thinly sliced

Salt and Pepper

STEP 1

For the egg mixture, whisk together the eggs, milk, green chilies, thyme, salt and pepper. In a casserole dish, layer the sliced baguette to fit; making two rows and tuck in ham slices between the baguette. Pour the egg mix over the baguette. Top with cheese, green onions and cilantro.

STEP 2

Bake at 350° until set, about 25 minutes.

BREAKFAST

FRENCH TOAST PUFFS

SO FANCY...

MOM TIP

Don't line the muffin tins with paper cups, you want to dip the top and bottom in the melted butter. These are perfect for freezing.

MAKES 12   **OVEN**   **25 MINUTES**   **$**

INGREDIENTS

1 box Plain Muffin Mix

¼ teaspoon Nutmeg

2 teaspoon Vanilla Extract

1 stick Butter, melted

¾ cup Sugar

2 teaspoon Cinnamon

DIRECTIONS

STEP 1

Assemble muffin batter according to directions, but also add nutmeg and vanilla. Mix well. Fill muffin tin and bake as directed.

STEP 2

While muffins are baking, melt butter. In another bowl, mix sugar and cinnamon.

STEP 3

Cool muffins until easy to handle, but still warm. Hold each muffin, and alternate dipping the tops and bottoms in butter. Then roll in cinnamon sugar mixture.

HUEVOS RANCHEROS

• RANCHER'S EGGS •

1-2 PERSON **20 MINUTES** **STOVETOP**

MOM TIP

Everyone usually thinks Huevos Rancheros take a long time to make, but they really don't! This recipe would serve 1–2 people, so adjust accordingly. These are not only a perfect breakfast dish, they make a great dinner, too!

INGREDIENTS

2 Corn Tortillas

2 Eggs

⅓– ½ Cup Refried Beans

⅓– ½ Cup Cheddar Cheese, shredded

2 Tablesppoons Green or Red Salsa

Additional toppings - Cilantro, Sour Cream, Avocado

DIRECTIONS

STEP 1

Heat up a medium frying pan and fry your eggs according to how you like them. Season with a little salt and pepper. Either microwave the beans or warm in a small pot. Warm tortillas over a stove flame to get them a little charred, or add them to a hot skillet with a little bit of oil until almost crisp.

STEP 2

To assemble, Spread some beans on the tortilla and top with cheese, then add the egg. Top with salsa and avocado. Add any other topping you would like.

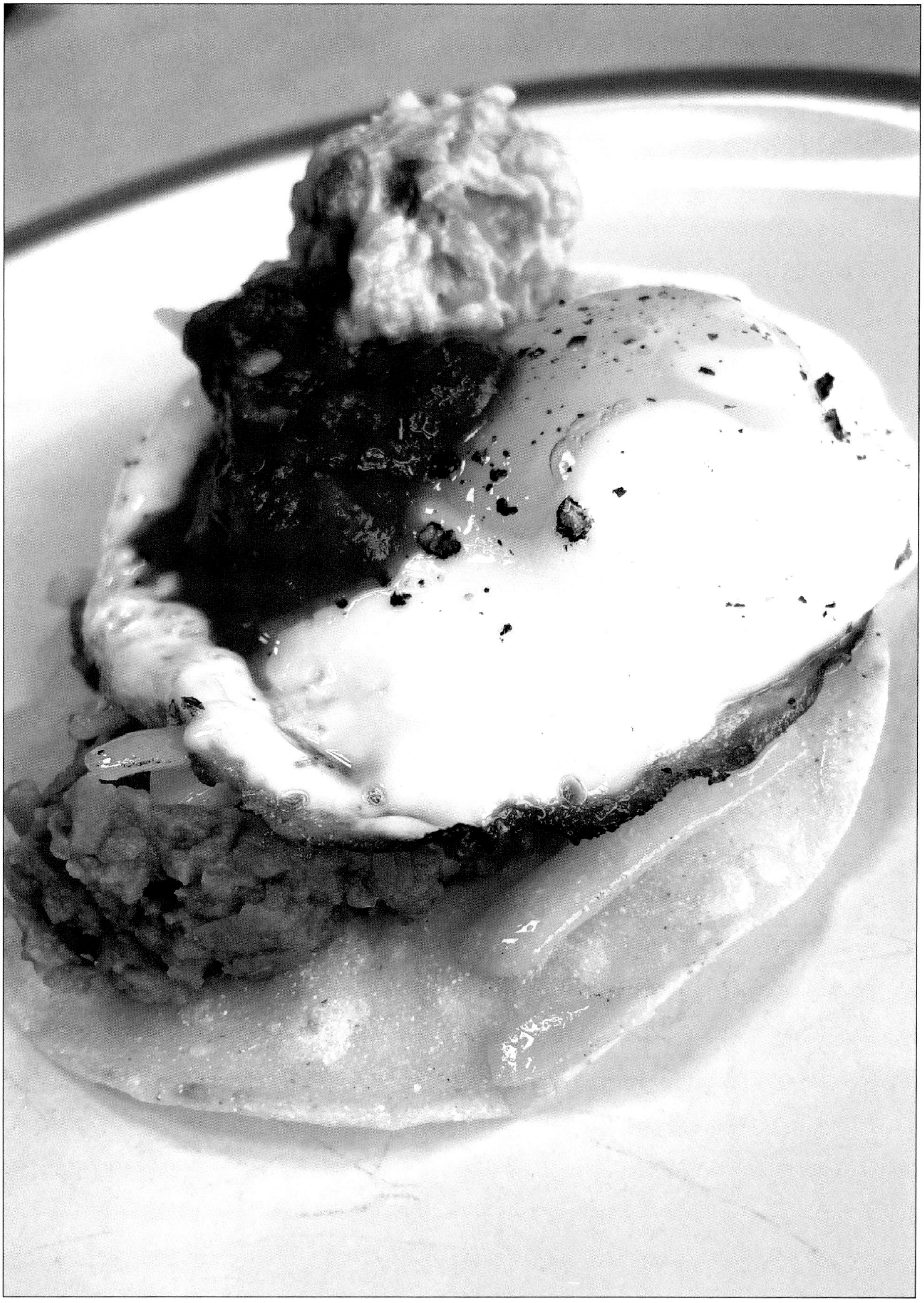

SOUPS & SIDES

SOUP INGREDIENTS

4 Carrots, peeled and chopped to large bite size pieces

2 Large Potatoes, peeled and diced into large bite size pieces

½ cup Onion, diced

6 cups Chicken Broth

2 Tablespoons Tomato Sauce

1 Tablespoon Dried Cilantro, or
¼ cup Fresh Cilantro

| 6 PERSON | STOVETOP | 50 MINUTES | $ |

ALBONDIGAS
SOUP

These pair well with quesadillas. Add a tortilla to an oiled hot frying pan over medium heat, add cheese of your choice. Fold in half and flip a time or two.

MEATBALL INGREDIENTS

1-½ lbs Lean Ground Sirloin

½ Cup Regular Long Grain White Rice, Uncooked

1 teaspoon Salt

1 teaspoon Pepper

1 teaspoon Garlic Powder

1 teaspoon Onion Powder

½ teaspoon Oregano

DIRECTIONS

STEP 1

Mix together beef, rice, salt, pepper, garlic powder, onion powder and oregano. Form into golf ball sized meatballs. Add to a large pot over medium heat. Add chicken broth, tomato sauce, carrots, potatoes, onion, meatballs and cilantro. Bring to a boil and reduce to a simmer. Continue to simmer for 30—40 minutes or until rice is fully cooked when a meatball is cut in half. Taste and adjust with salt and pepper.

POSOLE
EASY SOUP

MOM TIP

The toppings are what make this dish so flavorful- don't forget at least the lime and oregano.

8 PERSON **STOVETOP** **6-8 HOURS** **$$**

TOPPING IDEAS

Freshly Chopped Cilantro

Lime Wedges

Dried Oregano

Avocado & Sour Cream

Warm Tortillas

INGREDIENTS

1 "Tube" Of Chorizo

4 Center Cut Pork Chops (Or 4 Cups Pork Loin, Cut In Large Cubes)

8 cups Chicken Broth

2 (15 oz Cans) Hominy, drained

¼ cup Canned Green Chili

1 teaspoon Cumin

1 teaspoon Salt

1 teaspoon Onion Powder

1 teaspoon Garlic Powder

1 Tablespoon Oregano

DIRECTIONS

STEP 1

Add everything to a crock pot and cook for 6—8 hours on low until fork tender.

STEP 2

Remove pork and shred into large chunks. Add back to soup. Serve with fresh cilantro, lime wedges, dried oregano, and warm tortillas on the side.

TACO
SOUP

MOM TIP

Perfect to serve a crowd...In a pinch you can **make your own taco seasoning** mix with:
1 Tablespoon-Chili Powder,
1 Tablespoon-Salt,
1 teaspoon-Cumin,
1 Tablespoon-Onion Powder,
1 Tablespoon-Garlic Powder
1 Tablespoon-Oregano.

6 PERSON **STOVETOP** **40 MINUTES** **$$**

INGREDIENTS

1 can Stewed Tomatoes

3 Tablespoons Tomato Sauce

1 can Red Kidney Beans

½ pound Ground Sirloin

¼ cup Onion, diced

½ cup Frozen Corn

1 package Taco Seasoning

1 teaspoon Chili Powder

1 cup Cheddar Cheese, shredded

Sour Cream

Tortilla Chips

DIRECTIONS

STEP 1

Brown sirloin with onions and drain. Add taco seasoning, let sit for a couple minutes for the sauce to thicken. Add tomato sauce, stewed tomatoes, beans, corn, and chili powder. Bring to a boil. Add water, if needed, to desired consistency. Serve with cheddar cheese and sour cream. Dip with chips.

MOM TIP

This is a quick version of the classic Thai soup. Slicing the chicken very thin also helps in the speedy process.

TOM KHA GAI
SOUP

6 PERSON **20 MINUTES** **STOVETOP**

INGREDIENTS

1 cup White Rice

1 Tablespoon Olive Oil

½ Onion, sliced

½ teaspoon Ground Ginger

1 teaspoon Powdered Garlic

½ Jalapeño, sliced very thin

3 Tablespoons Fresh Squeeze Lime Juice (About One Lime)

1 teaspoon Thai Red or Green Curry Paste

1 - (14 ½ ounce) Canned Coconut Milk

3 cups Chicken Broth

2 Boneless Skinless Chicken Breasts, sliced into thin bite-size pieces

1 cup Mushrooms, sliced thin

¼ cup Chopped Cilantro

¼ teaspoon Chili Flakes

DIRECTIONS

STEP 1

Cook 1 cup rice in water using your favorite method. While that is cooking: Follow step 2.

STEP 2

In a medium pot heat the olive oil over medium heat add the onion and stir until softened. Add the ginger, garlic, jalapeño, 2 Tablespoons cilantro, coconut milk and chicken broth. Add lime juice and chili flakes to taste. Add chicken and mushrooms and lightly simmer for about 20 minutes. Add lime juice and chili flakes to taste.

STEP 3

To serve, scoop about half cup rice in the bottom of your bowl. Ladle soup over rice and top with chopped cilantro, green onion, mushrooms, and a lime wedge on the side.

VEGGIE CORN CHOWDER

VEGETARIAN

MOM TIP

You can change this to so many options. Feel free to add chopped cooked bacon, diced ham, or sautéed veggies, or a different type of cheese.

INGREDIENTS

2 Tablespoons Butter

1 Tablespoon Olive Oil

1 Small Onion, diced

1 Red Bell Pepper, diced

1 cup Chopped Celery

1 cup Chopped Red Potato

1 cup Carrot, sliced

1—16 ounce bag frozen corn
(baby corn or sweet corn)

½ teaspoon Pepper

1 teaspoon Salt

¼ teaspoon Dried Thyme

2—4 Tablespoons Chopped Green Chilies (optional)

2 cups Chicken Broth

1½ cups Heavy Cream

1½ cups Cheddar Cheese, shredded

4-6 PERSON   **STOVETOP**   **30 MINUTES**   **$**

DIRECTIONS

STEP 1

Heat butter and olive oil in a pot and add onion, celery, carrots and bell pepper. Sauté until onions are translucent. Add seasonings, potatoes, corn and stir to combine. Add chicken broth (adding more liquid if needed), just to cover vegetables.

STEP 2

Gently simmer for 20—30 minutes until potatoes are soft. Add cream and bring to a hard simmer. Cook until slightly thickened. Turn off heat and add cheese.

ZUPPA TOSCANA

SUPER EASY PREP.

MOM TIP

This hearty soup is also so good the next day.

4 PERSON   **STOVETOP**   **45 MINUTES**   **$$**

COOK LIKE MOM

INGREDIENTS ●────────────────●

4 Slices Bacon, chopped

2 Tablespoons Olive Oil

1 Onion, chopped

1 lb Fresh Sweet Italian Sausage,
casing removed

2 Potatoes, peeled and sliced

4-5 cups Chicken Broth

1 cup Heavy Cream

1 cup Fresh Kale, chopped

½ teaspoon Chili Flakes, dried

DIRECTIONS

STEP 1 ●────────────────

In a large pot over medium high heat, add chopped bacon to the olive oil and cook until crispy. Remove bacon with a slotted spoon. Add the chopped onion to the oil along with the sweet Italian sausage. Cook until sausage begins to brown. Then add the sliced potatoes and 4 cups chicken broth. Continue to cook until potatoes are tender (adding more chicken broth if necessary) about 25 minutes.

STEP 2 ●────────────────

Add heavy cream, chopped kale and continue to cook about 5–10 more minutes or until flavors have blended and kale has wilted down. Add bacon back to soup, add chili flakes and taste to adjust seasonings with salt and pepper.

ASPARAGUS BUNDLES

PARTY IN A POUCH

MOM TIP

Such an easy side dish if you're using the grill. These can also be broiled, but you have to keep your eye on them so they don't burn.

4 PERSON   **GRILL**   **15 MINUTES**   **$**

INGREDIENTS

1 bunch Asparagus, cleaned and trimmed

4 slices Bacon

DIRECTIONS

STEP 1

Divide the asparagus into 4 bundles. Wrap a piece of bacon around bundles. Grill, turning to brown the bacon evenly.

BRUSCHETTA
• TO TOAST •

2 PERSON   **10 MINUTES**   **BROILER**

MOM TIP

For a heartier take on bruschetta, top it with some blue cheese and set under the broiler until melted (pictured with and without cheese).

INGREDIENTS

1—12" Baguette

1 container Little Baby Tomatoes

¼ cup Fresh Basil, chopped

2 Tablespoons Olive Oil

2 Tablespoons Balsamic Vinegar

2 Cloves Garlic, peeled

Salt and Pepper

Parmesan Cheese

DIRECTIONS

STEP 1

Chop tomatoes. Place tomatoes and chopped fresh basil in a bowl and drizzle a little oil and vinegar to coat. Add salt and pepper to taste. Slice baguette in thick slices. Broil or toast pieces on both sides until golden brown. Rub garlic gently on split side with a whole garlic clove. Discard the rest of the garlic. Top baguette with tomato mixture.

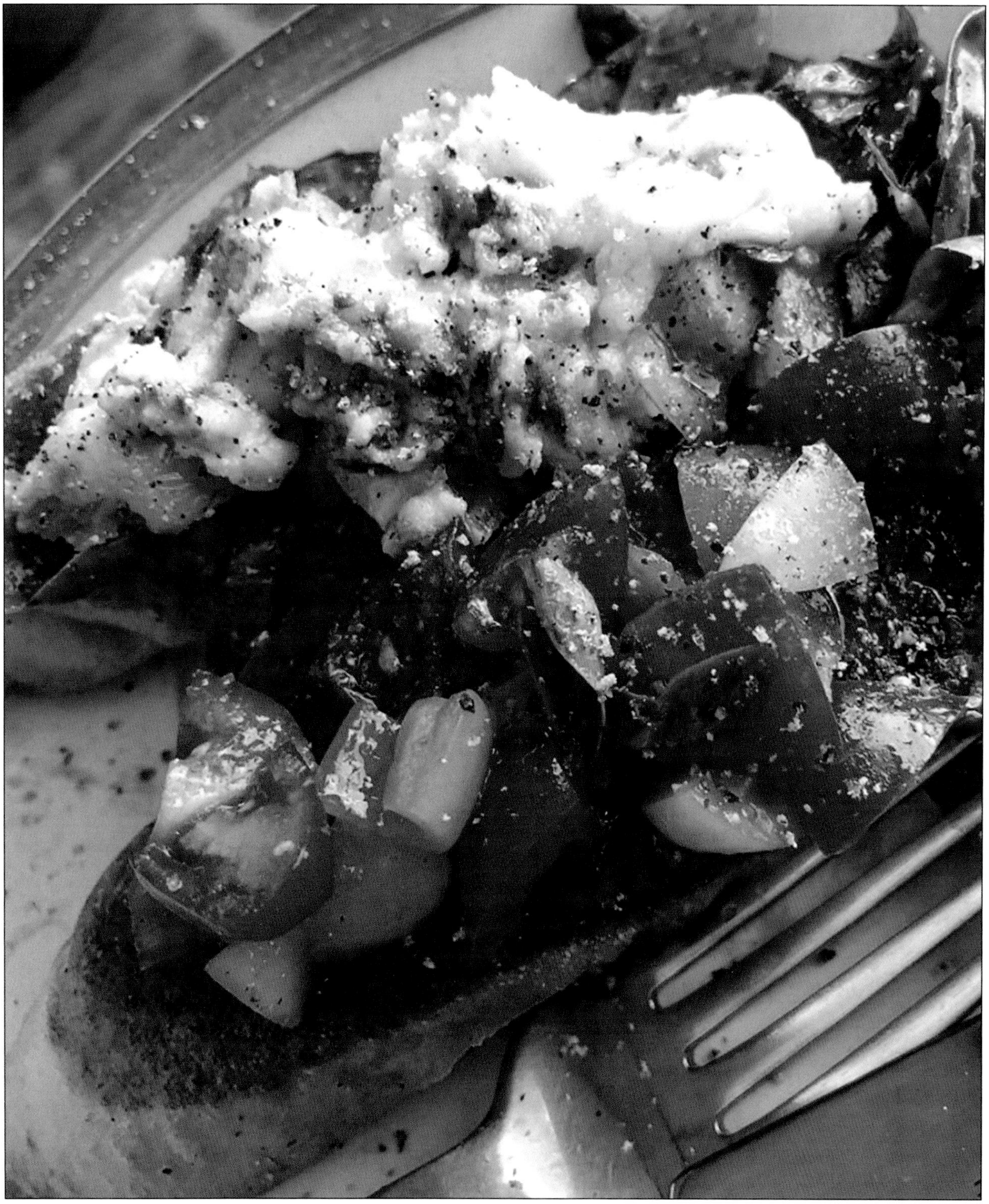

DIRECTIONS

STEP 1 ●────────────────

Prepare Corn by grill - place corn in husks over grill for about 4 minutes each side until husks are browned.

Prepare Corn by boiling- Remove husk and silk and place in boiling water for about 5 minutes, turning a few times so all sides are cooked.

STEP 2 ●────────────────

Once cooked corn is cooled, remove all husk and silk and cut off from the cob using a knife or a mandolin. Mix with all ingredients and keep chilled until ready to serve.

INGREDIENTS

2 ears of Fresh Corn- Grilled or Boiled

½ cup Red Bell Pepper, diced

1 Jalapeño, minced

¼ cup Red Onion, thinly sliced

½ cup Grape Tomatoes, cut in half

½ cup Fresh Parsley, chopped (or cilantro)

½ cup Crumbled Feta Cheese

½ lime, juiced

3 Tablespoons Olive Oil

1 Tablespoon Red Wine Vinegar

Salt and Pepper

CORN SALAD

SUMMER BASICS.

MOM TIP

This recipe is great to substitute or add whatever vegetables you like! Bottled Italian dressing also works well.

| 4 PERSON | STOVETOP | 15 MINUTES | $ |

CLASSIC RISOTTO
ITALIAN BASICS.

MOM TIP

I love making this dish. Amounts aren't exact because you slowly add the broth until the rice is soft and to your liking. It's a filling dish and you can add any vegetables you want. My favorite is butternut squash and bacon, but you can add peas, mushrooms or asparagus. Takes some time to make, but it's so worth it!

6-8 PERSON   **STOVETOP**   **40 MINUTES**   **$$**

INGREDIENTS

2 Tablespoons Olive Oil

½ cup Onion, diced

1 cup (Optional) of your Favorite Vegetable, sliced or chopped

1 ½ cup Arborio Rice

½ cup White Wine

5—6 cups Chicken Broth

½ teaspoon Dried Thyme

About ½ cup Grated Parmesan Cheese, plus more for serving

¼ teaspoon Salt and Pepper

DIRECTIONS

STEP 1 •————————————

Heat the broth in a pot on the stove until hot. Set aside but keep warm. To a large sauce pan over medium heat, sauté onion in olive oil until soft. (Add your vegetable of choice and sauté for about a minute more.) Season with salt and pepper. Add the rice next and using a wooden spoon mix until all the rice is coated with some of the oil. Add half of the wine and scrape the bottom of the pan to deglaze and remove any stuck bits in the pan.

STEP 2 •————————————

Turn down the saucepan to medium low and start adding the broth ½ cup at a time. Between each addition, constantly but slowly stir the rice. When all the liquid is absorbed, add another ½ cup. Continue this method until the rice is cooked through but still has a bite to it (like al dente pasta). When you get to this point, turn heat up to medium. Add the remaining white wine and mix until evaporated, about a minute. turn heat down to low and add parmesan cheese. Mix gently to combine.

CREAMY POLENTA

MOM TIP

This is another fast, filling and simple recipe. This can be a side dish to your fanciest of entrées. Experiment with different cheeses or herbs and see what is your favorite.

4-6 PERSON   **STOVE**   **50 MINUTES**   **$**

INGREDIENTS

2½ cups Water

1 cup Heavy Cream

1 cup Yellow Polenta

1 teaspoon Salt

¼ teaspoon Pepper

½ teaspoon Fresh Thyme Leaves **or**

¼ teaspoon Dried Thyme

¼ cup Parmesan Cheese, grated

1 teaspoon Lemon Zest

DIRECTIONS

STEP 1

Simmer water in a medium pot. Whisk in polenta and continue to gently simmer until polenta has thickened, about 5–10 minutes. Whisk in heavy cream and continue to cook until slightly thickened, about another minute. Stir in seasonings, cheese and lemon zest.

MEXICAN ELOTE
• STREETFOOD REMIX •

4 PERSON   15 MINUTES   GRILL

MOM TIP

You can peel the corn and place in foil to grill or do like me and just place unpeeled corn on the grill. A fun way to serve is to cut the corn in half and skewer each corn.

INGREDIENTS

4 Corn On The Cobs

¼ cup Mayonnaise

½ cup Mexican Cotija Cheese

Chili Powder and Salt

Limes

DIRECTIONS

STEP 1

Grill corn, remove husks, and rub with mayonnaise. Roll in crumbled cheese, then add a couple dashes of chili powder. Finish by squeezing a lime wedge over.

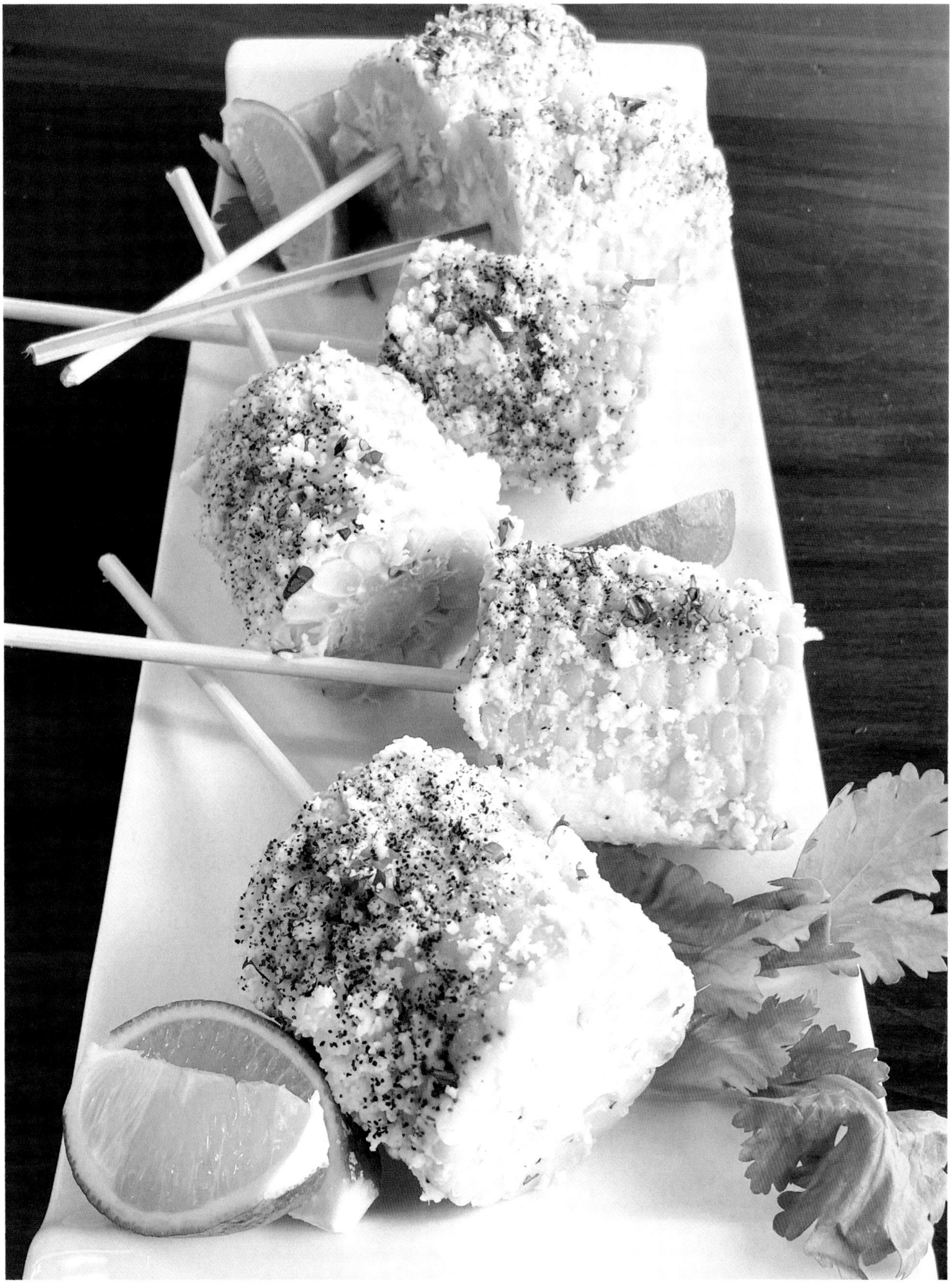

GRANDMA'S MEXICAN RICE

FAMILY FAVOURITE

MOM TIP

Use this rice as a side dish or add into breakfast burritos! I like using it for taco salads too.

6 PERSON

STOVETOP

25 MINUTES

$

INGREDIENTS

1 Tablespoon Olive Oil

¼ cup Yellow Onion, chopped

1 cup White Rice

2 cups Chicken Broth

2 Tablespoons Tomato Sauce

2 Tablespoons Cilantro

1 Green Onion, chopped

DIRECTIONS

STEP 1

To a medium pan over medium heat, sauté onion in olive oil until soft. Add the rice to the pan and stir until fragrant and parts of the rice are a little golden. Next step, Add the chicken broth, tomato sauce, cilantro and green onion and stir to combine. Raise the heat to medium-high and cook until the broth starts to boil. As soon as it starts to boil, cover pan with a lid, reduce heat to low, and cook for about 20—25 minutes. Check at 20 minutes; there should be no liquid remaining. Fluff with a fork and serve.

4 PERSON   **STOVETOP**   **20 MINUTES**   **$**

INGREDIENTS

1 cup Cheddar Cheese, grated

3 cups Water

½ teaspoon Salt

1 cup Corn Grits

DIRECTIONS

STEP 1

Bring water and salt to a boil in a medium pot. Add corn grits and reduce heat to low. Cook for about 5 minutes, stirring occasionally, until liquid is absorbed and grits are creamy. Add in cheese and stir until melted.

GRITS W/ CHEESE

QUICK & EASY.

MOM TIP

Makes a delicious hearty side dish and it's very quick and inexpensive.
These are great for breakfast as well.

POTATO STACKS

SO FANCY.

MOM TIP

These little gems are easy to make with whatever type of potato you use. If you have a mandolin or a food processor with the slicing blade, use it!

6-8 PERSON **OVEN** **30 MINUTES** **$**

INGREDIENTS

6 cups Potatoes, thinly sliced

¼— ⅓ cup Olive Oil

¼ cup Green Onions, Chives or Parsley minced

2 Cloves Garlic, crushed & minced

1 teaspoon Fresh Thyme
or ¼ teaspoon Dried Thyme

1 teaspoon Salt

¼ teaspoon Pepper

DIRECTIONS

STEP 1

In a large bowl, combine potatoes, onions, garlic and seasonings. Add enough olive oil to thoroughly coat potatoes, making sure all sides of the potato slices are coated.

Place stacks of potatoes in a muffin tin to keep the "stack" shape.

STEP 2

Bake at 375° until fork tender, about 25 minutes.

THE COOKBOOK

MAINS

PAN SEARED STEAK
SAVOURY

MOM TIP

Pan Searing a steak creates an amazing crust! A cast iron skillet is nice because it can get very hot. I like to buy a nice sized steak and cut into slices to serve 2 people. A meat thermometer is handy to use before removing from the pan so you know your steak is cooked the way you like it.

2-PERSON

STOVE

30 MINUTES

$$$

INGREDIENTS

Any steak you would usually grill, with or without bone, about 1 ½ −2" thick

Olive Oil (or avocado, grapeseed oil)

Salt and Pepper

2 Tablespoons Butter

2 Cloves Garlic, smashed

4 Sprigs Thyme

1 Sprig Rosemary

DIRECTIONS

STEP 1

Season the steak heavily with salt and pepper. Heat a pan over high heat until very hot. Pat the steak dry and add about 2 Tablespoons oil to the pan. Place steak in skillet and cook 2 ½ minutes each side (for medium rare). Reduce heat to low and add the butter, garlic, thyme and rosemary. Tilt the pan so the butter and herbs pool to one area. Using a spoon, baste the steak with the butter, garlic and herbs for about 30 seconds. Remove steak and let rest about 5 minutes before slicing.

CHEESEBURGER MACARONI

FEED THE CROWD

MOM TIP

Cook the pasta while you are frying the beef and making sauce. You can do it all on the stove at the same time.

4-6 PERSON   **STOVETOP**   **25 MINUTES**   **$$**

INGREDIENTS

1 pound Ground Sirloin

12 oz Elbow Macaroni

1 Tablespoon Butter

1 Tablespoon Flour

1 ¼ cup Milk

2 cups Sharp Cheddar Cheese, Shredded

¼ teaspoon Onion Powder

¼ teaspoon Garlic Powder

Salt and Pepper

DIRECTIONS

STEP 1

Cook macaroni according to directions. Drain and set aside. Meanwhile, in a large skillet over medium high heat, cook the beef with salt, pepper, onion and garlic powders. Cook until completely brown. Drain any fat and remove.

STEP 2

To a medium pot over medium heat, sauté onion in butter until tender. Season with salt and pepper. Stir in flour and whisk for about a minute, stirring constantly. Add milk all at once, stirring with a whisk until combined and cook until thickened and bubbly. Lower heat to low, add shredded cheese and stir until melted. Add the cheese sauce and the beef to the cooked macaroni and stir gently until combined.

CROCK POT BRISKET

FAMILY FAVOURITE

MOM TIP

You can use this brisket in so many things! From enchiladas, salads, sandwiches, paninis, and soups... to on its own over some rice. Freeze any leftovers for the next time. This might be more expensive to buy, but it makes a lot so you can get mulitple meals out of it. Sweet & Smoky BBQ recipe on page 107...

Sweet & Smoky BBQ recipe on page 107...

MAKES A LOT   **CROCKPOT**   **6-8 HOURS**   **$$$**

COOK LIKE MOM

DIRECTIONS

INGREDIENTS

2–3 lbs Flat Cut Beef Brisket

1 cup Beef Broth or Water

1 Tablespoon Liquid Smoke

1 Tablespoon Salt

1 teaspoon Garlic Powder

2 teaspoons Onion Powder

½ teaspoon Pepper

STEP 1

Place brisket & broth in crockpot, fat side up. (You may have to cut the brisket in half to make fit.) Season the top of the brisket with all of the seasonings. Cover and cook on low for about 6–8 hours, or until brisket shreds easily with two forks.

STEP 2

Remove the brisket from crock pot, cut fat top off and remove. Shred with two forks and place shredded brisket back in crock pot juices until ready to serve.

SOUTHERN LOW BOIL
TALK ABOUT FLAVOR.

MOM TIP

Serve this on large pieces of butcher paper right on the table. Makes for a fun and easy party menu. Crusty French Bread would be great to serve on the side.

MAKES A LOT GRILL/STOVE 30 MINUTES $$

INGREDIENTS

3 Boneless Chicken Breasts

12 Large Uncooked Shrimp w/ shell on

3 Links of Andouille Sausage

3 Ears Corn, husked, broken into thirds

20 Baby Potatoes

Old Bay Seasoning

3 Limes cut into wedges

¼ cup Butter, melted

DIRECTIONS

STEP 1 •————————

Season the chicken with salt, pepper and Old Bay seasoning. In a medium bowl, toss the shrimp with melted butter, and season with Old Bay seasoning. Heat a large pot with water and add about 1/4 cup Old Bay seasoning. Fire up the grill.

STEP 2 •————————

To the boiling water, add the potatoes for 5 minutes, then add the corn. Continue to cook until potatoes are fork tender.

To the grill, cook the chicken, shrimp and sausage until all are cooked, squeezing a few lime wedges over as you cook. Slice the chicken and Andouille into bite size pieces. Toss everything together before tossing onto the table to serve. Garnish with sliced limes.

LINDA'S MEATLOAF
SUNDAY DINNER

MOM TIP

If you don't have breadcrumbs, you can finely chop bread or crackers.

INGREDIENTS

½ cup Bread Crumbs

¾ cup Onion, minced

¼ cup Celery, minced

¼ cup Bell Pepper, diced

2 Eggs

2 lbs Ground Sirloin

2 Tablespoons Salsa

2 Tablespoons Horseradish

1 teaspoon Salt

1 teaspoon Dry Mustard

¼ cup Milk

¼ cup Ketchup, plus more for top

DIRECTIONS

STEP 1

Combine all ingredients together, being gentle when mixing. Shape into a loaf on lightly greased pan with sides. Coat meatloaf with a thin layer of ketchup. Bake at 350° for 35–45 minutes or until cooked through. Let sit for a few minutes before slicing.

6 PERSON   **OVEN**   **1 HOUR**   **$$**

MONGOLIAN BEEF

ASIAN INSPIRED.

MOM TIP

Don't add too much salt to the flank steak when seasoning because soy sauce is salty. Make sure to cut across the grain of the flank steak.

| 4 PERSON | STOVETOP | 40 MINUTES | $$ |

INGREDIENTS

1 teaspoon Powdered Ginger

½ teaspoon Garlic Powder

⅓ cup Soy Sauce or Tamari Sauce

⅓ cup Water

½ cup Brown Sugar

2 Tablespoons Oil (Add More If Needed For Frying)

1 ½ lbs Flank Steak, Sliced Thin Across The Grain In About One Inch Length Pieces

2 Tablespoons Cornstarch

1—2 cups Broccoli Flowerettes

3 Sliced Green Onions

DIRECTIONS

STEP 1 ●————————————

Cook rice according to directions. Meanwhile, slice up the flank steak and lightly season with salt and pepper. Toss sliced flank steak and cornstarch together. In a small bowl, mix together the ginger, garlic, soy, brown sugar, and water. Set aside. Heat a large frying pan on high, coat with oil and add the flank steak. Quickly fry the beef until it's just brown (because you'll cook it again in the sauce). You might have to fry the beef in two batches so it isn't too crowded in the pan. Remove each batch as you go. When the steak is all cooked and out of the pan, add broccoli and onion and sauté until just crisp tender about a minute.

STEP 2 ●————————————

Return the steak back to the pan with the broccoli and add the sauce to the pan. Bring to a boil and continue to cook on high until sauce is thickened. Toss to coat. Serve over cooked rice.

PASTA RAPIDO

4 PERSON | **10 MINUTES** | **STOVETOP**

MOM TIP

You will be done making this before the pasta is cooked! Adding chopped cooked chicken would make for a quick and easy dinner.

INGREDIENTS

1 package Pasta Noodles, Fettuccini

½ cup Olive Oil

1 cup Italian Parsley, chopped

½ teaspoon Chili Flakes

1 teaspoon Salt

Parmesan Cheese, if desired

DIRECTIONS

STEP 1

Cook pasta according to directions. While that is cooking, warm the olive oil in a medium pan over medium heat. Add the parsley, salt and chili flakes. Let cook for about a minute or two. Adjust seasonings and toss with cooked pasta. Top with Parmesan, if desired.

ROPA VIEJA
A CUBAN LOVE

MOM TIP

This is super easy, just add it all to a crock pot and turn it on. I like to serve this with rice and a few mentioned toppings below. You can serve leftovers in a warmed tortilla. Traditional Cuban dinners always have cooked black beans with this— you can warm a can of beans as a quick and easy side!

COOK LIKE MOM

INGREDIENTS

2 lbs Flank Steak

½ Onion, Sliced

1 Carrot, Peeled and Diced

1 Red Bell Pepper, Seeded and Sliced

1 Small Can Tomato Paste

1 can Diced Tomatoes

½ cup Green Olives with Pimento, Sliced

2 cups Chicken Broth

1 teaspoon Salt

½ teaspoon Pepper

½ teaspoon Onion Powder

½ teaspoon Garlic Powder

1 Tablespoon Dried Oregano

1 teaspoon Cumin Powder

1 Tablespoon Red Wine Vinegar

2 Bay Leaves

Cooked White Rice

GARNISHES- Fresh chopped cilantro, Fresh minced onion, Fresh Lime wedges.

6-8 PERSON **CROCKPOT** **5-7 HOURS** **$$**

DIRECTIONS

STEP 1 •————————

Add all the ingredients (except rice and garnishes) into a crock pot and cook on low for about 5—7 hours or until beef shreds easily using two forks. Remove the beef and shred. Return the shredded beef back to the crockpot sauce.

STEP 2 •————————

Serve with white rice, cilantro, minced onions, and lime wedges.

THE COOKBOOK

SAUSAGE, BELL PEPPERS & ONIONS

SHARING IS CARING

MOM TIP

Just a small handful of fresh herbs makes a difference! When using fresh thyme, one sprig will be enough. I love to serve this over Polenta, or even topped with some spaghetti sauce and tucked into some crusty french rolls for a sandwich.

2 PERSON **STOVETOP** **20 MINUTES** **$$**

INGREDIENTS

4 Sweet Italian Sausages

½ Onion, sliced

2 Bell Peppers, sliced

3 Tablespoons Olive Oil

Parsley, Chives, Fresh Thyme- Optional

Salt and Pepper to Taste

DIRECTIONS

STEP 1

In a large skillet over medium heat, add the oil and sausages. Sauté about 2–3 minutes each side, about 10 minutes total. Add the bell peppers and onions to the sausages (and fresh herbs if you'd like). Season with salt and pepper. Cook about 5 minutes while stirring occasionally. Cover with a lid and continue to cook another minute or two.

BEEF STEW
ULTIMATE COMFORT

6 PERSON

CROCKPOT

5–7 HOURS

$$

MOM TIP

Makes a lot and tastes even better the next day. This cooks well in a 325° oven for 3 hours. Cover the pot with foil or a tight fitting lid.

TYPE OF WINE YOU CAN SERVE:

- Shiraz

- Merlot

- Pinot Noir

INGREDIENTS

3 lbs Beef Chuck, cubed bite sized

2—3 cups Baby Red Potatoes

2—3 cups Baby or Peeled Carrots. chopped

1 cup Celery or Mushrooms, diced

1 Onion, diced

1 cup of Red Wine

2 cups Beef Broth

2 teaspoons Salt

1 teaspoon Pepper

2 teaspoons Onion Powder

1 teaspoon Garlic Powder

2 Tablespoons Cornstarch

DIRECTIONS

STEP 1

Add all ingredients **except** for cornstarch. Turn crockpot on low and cook for about 5-7 hours until the beef can easily fall apart when pierced.

Mix the cornstarch in ¼ cup cold water until smooth, otherwise, will turn out lumpy.

Add to crockpot and stir until thickened. Taste and adjust seasonings to your liking.

SUNDAY GRAVY
TALK ABOUT FLAVOR.

MOM TIP

Excellent for leftovers... This is one of those meals that even tastes better the second day, plus it freezes well and makes a lot!

MAKES A LOT   CROCKPOT   5–7 HOURS $$$

INGREDIENTS

1 Large Onion, chopped

4 Garlic Cloves, minced

3–28 oz Cans Crushed Tomatoes

1 lb Flank Steak

1 lb Beef Country Ribs

1 lb Fresh Sweet Italian Sausage

1 lb Fresh Spicy Italian Sausage

1 teaspoon Garlic Powder

1 teaspoon Onion Powder

1 teaspoon Dried Basil

1 teaspoon Dried Oregano

1 teaspoon Dried Thyme

1 teaspoon Salt

1 teaspoon Pepper

Cooked Pasta

Parmesan Cheese for Serving

DIRECTIONS

STEP 1

Add all ingredients except pasta and cheese, into a large crockpot and cover with lid. Cook on low for about 5–7 hours or until flank steak shreds easily. Before serving, remove flank steak, ribs and sausages. Shred flank steak and ribs (discarding any bones or fat) and slice the sausages. Add back to sauce and stir gently to combine.

STEP 2

Serve over pasta of your choice and top with Parmesan cheese.

BEEF SHORT RIBS

SUPER FANCY

MOM TIP

Short ribs are not expensive and super easy to make. The oven does all the work with the slow and low bake. The outcome is amazing and you could serve this to the fanciest of guests! Serve this over polenta, grits, rice or pasta.

INGREDIENTS

3 Tablespoons Olive Oil

8 Short Ribs Of Beef

Salt and Pepper

1 Onion, chopped

2 Ribs Celery, chopped

2 Carrots, chopped

2 Garlic Cloves, chopped

1 teaspoon Salt

½ teaspoon Pepper

¼ teaspoon Dried Thyme
(Or A Few Sprigs Fresh)

3 Tablespoons Flour

3 Tablespoons Tomato Paste

3 cups Red Wine

1 cup Beef Broth

Fresh thyme sprigs for garnish (if you want to be fancy)

DIRECTIONS

Preheat oven to 325°.

Season short ribs with salt and pepper. In a large oven proof casserole dish, heat the olive oil and brown all sides of the short ribs, about a minute or two on each side. Remove the short ribs to a plate. Add the onion, celery, carrot and garlic and cook until soft. Add the flour and tomato paste and stir for about a minute.

Add the wine, broth, salt and pepper and stir to remove any stuck bits from the bottom of the pan. Remove from heat and add the ribs to the pot, nestling them all in the sauce.

Cover with a lid (you may need to add foil to the top before adding the lid to give it a tight fit). Add to oven and cook for about 3 hours or until the meat is fork tender.

Gently remove the beef and strain the sauce. Throw away the cooked vegetables. To serve, spoon some sauce over the ribs, garnish with a fresh thyme sprig.

4 PERSON   OVEN   3 HOURS $$

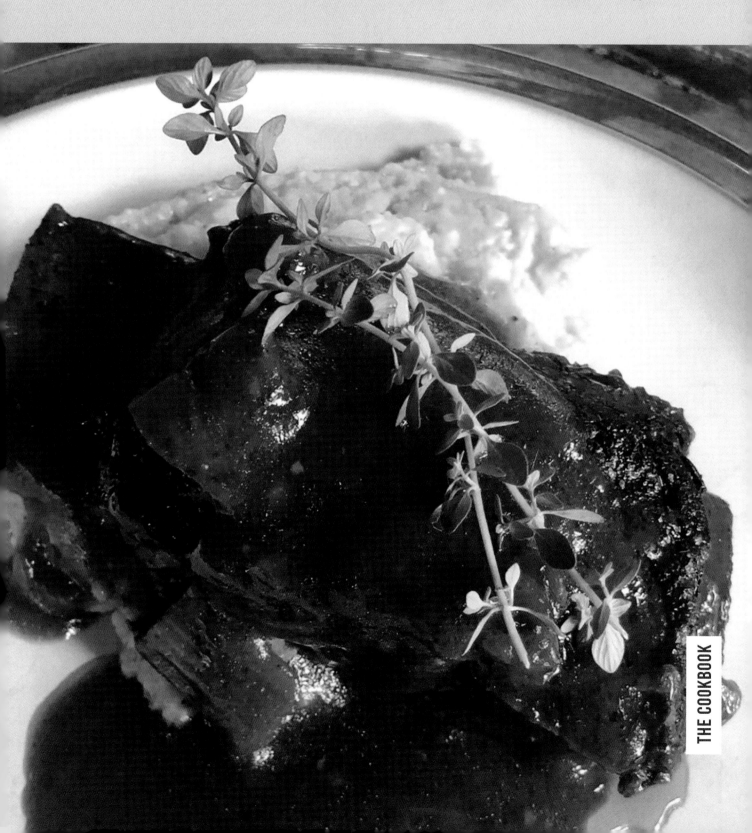

THE COOKBOOK

MACARONI & CHEESE

COMFORT FOOD.

MOM TIP

You can change this to so many options, by adding chopped cooked bacon, diced ham, or sautéed veggies, or a different type of cheese.

4 PERSON   **STOVETOP**   **15 MINUTES**   **$$**

COOK LIKE MOM

INGREDIENTS

1½ cup Elbow Macaroni, Dried

1 teaspoon Olive Oil

½ cup Onion, chopped

3 Tablespoons Butter

3 Tablespoon Flour

½ teaspoon Pepper

½ teaspoon Salt

2 cups Milk

2 cups Sharp Cheddar Cheese, shredded

3 Tablespoons Bread Crumbs

1 Tablespoon Butter (Optional if you want a crumb topping)

DIRECTIONS

STEP 1

Cook macaroni according to package directions. Meanwhile, make the cheese sauce: In a large saucepan, cook onions in olive oil until tender. Move onions to outside of pan and to the center, add butter. Melt. Stir flour into butter and add salt and pepper. Whisk and cook flour mixture one minute longer. Add milk all at once and continue to whisk until smooth. Stir with a wooden spoon over medium heat until mixture is thickened and creamy, about 2 minutes. Lower heat and stir in shredded cheese until melted. Gently mix cheese with cooked macaroni.

STEP 2

Pour into a casserole dish. If topping with bread crumbs, sprinkle bread crumbs over top of macaroni. Dot butter over casserole and bake uncovered at 350° for about 10 minutes or until topping is golden.

GARLIC BRAISED
• CHICKEN THIGHS •

4 PERSON   **2 HOURS**   **OVEN**

MOM TIP

Chicken thighs are inexpensive and really, way more flavorful than chicken breasts. Sometimes I add about 1/2 cup chorizo (in Tablespoons) to the skillet before covering and baking. I have also added a squeeze of lemon and a handful of peas right before serving. This is great over rice or mashed potatoes because it creates a lot of sauce while it cooks.

INGREDIENTS

8 Chicken Thighs, bone in & skin on

3 Tablespoons Olive Oil

3 Tablespoons Butter

1 Onion, sliced

2 Heads Garlic, peeled & gently smashed

Salt and Pepper

1 cup White Wine

½ cup Chicken Broth

½ teaspoon Thyme Leaves, or a few sprigs of fresh thyme

DIRECTIONS

STEP 1

Preheat oven to 325°. Pat chicken thighs dry and season with salt and pepper. To an oven proof skillet over medium high heat, add the olive oil and brown both sides of the thighs. When all thighs are browned, lower heat and add the butter, onions, garlic, white wine, chicken broth and thyme leaves. Cover tightly with foil or a lid and bake for about 1 1/2-2 hours or until chicken thighs fall off the bone easily.

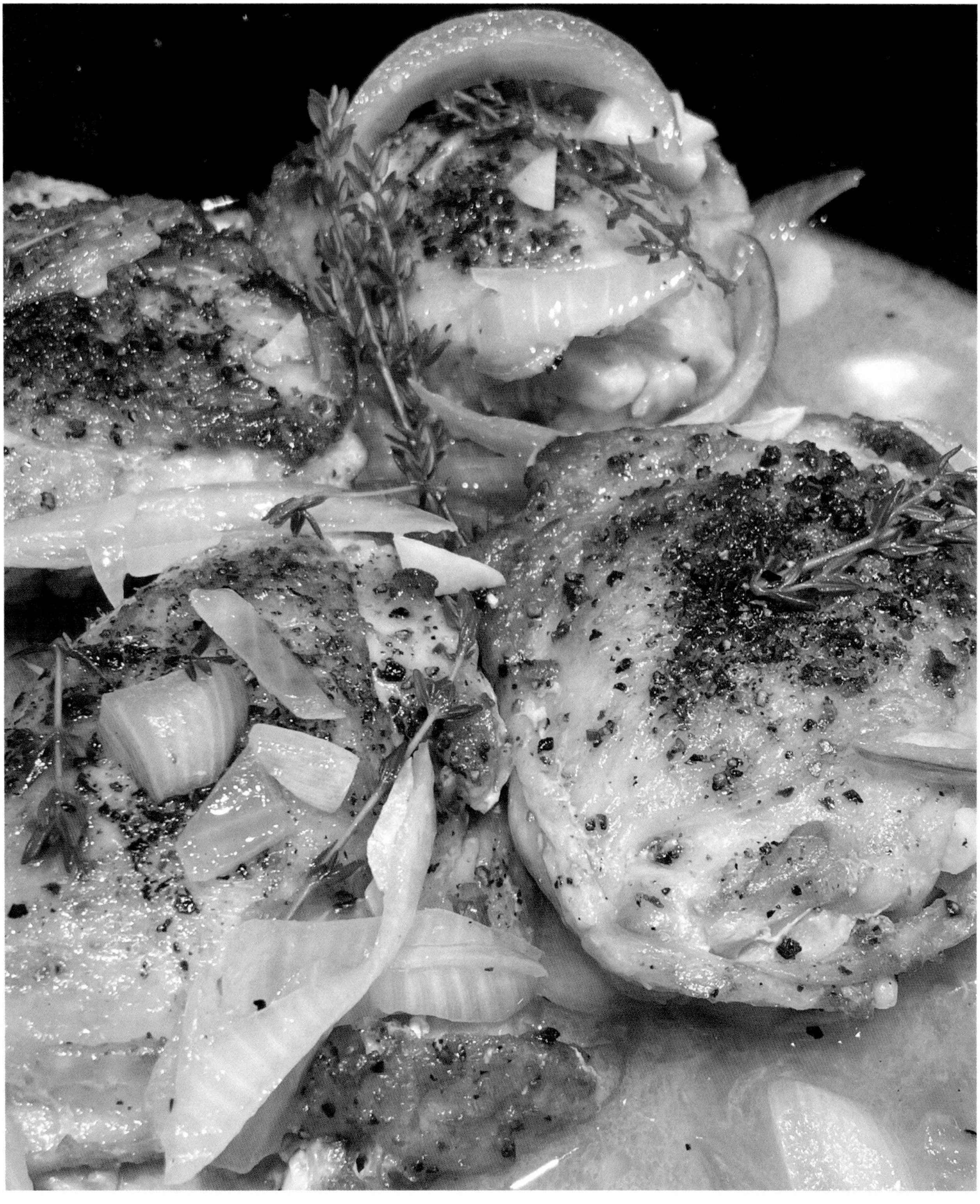

DIRECTIONS

STEP 1

Mix the flour, salt, pepper, garlic powder and onion powder together in a shallow bowl or plate. Pound chicken breasts until ½" thick. Dip the chicken breasts in the flour to dust lightly on both sides. Heat butter in a large skillet. Lightly brown chicken over medium high heat, about 5 minutes each side. Add the sliced mushrooms to chicken in the skillet, cover and cook for 10 minutes. Add heavy cream and simmer over low heat for 10 minutes. Remove just the chicken and keep warm on a dish.

STEP 2

Add champagne to the sauce in the skillet. Bring to a rapid boil, stirring occasionally and cook until sauce is reduced to a creamy consistency, 3 to 5 minutes. Season to taste with salt and pepper. Serve over chicken breasts.

INGREDIENTS

¼ cup Flour

¼ teaspoon Salt

⅛ teaspoon Pepper

¼ teaspoon Garlic Powder

¼ teaspoon Onion Powder

½ cup Butter

4 Boneless Skinless Chicken Breasts pounded

1 lb Mushrooms, sliced

1 cup Heavy Cream

¼ cup Champagne

Salt and Pepper

CHICKEN BREAST WITH CHAMPAGNE SAUCE
QUICK & EASY.

MOM TIP

This can be considered "fancy", but it's super easy to make. You can buy mini bottles of champagne (or you can also use white wine in a pinch). You can make this for me when you have me to dinner!.

4 PERSON   **STOVETOP**   **35 MINTUES**   **$$**

4 PERSON   STOVETOP   15 MINUTES $$

CHICKEN PARMESAN
AN ITALIAN FAVORITE

No one will ever know its a jar of spaghetti sauce!

INGREDIENTS

4 Chicken Breasts, pounded

1 Jar Spaghetti Sauce

Parmesan Cheese, shredded

1 package, Pasta (Spaghetti)

3 Tablespoons Olive Oil

DIRECTIONS

STEP 1

Cook pasta according to directions. Pound chicken breast to ½" thick. Season with salt and pepper. Fry chicken breasts in olive oil 5 minutes on each side or until cooked through.

STEP 2

Slice the chicken and warm the spaghetti sauce. To serve, place sliced chicken over pasta, top with sauce and parmesan cheese.

CHICKEN ENCHILADA CASSEROLE

QUICK & EASY.

MOM TIP

This has always been one of my quick go-to recipes and everyone loves it! You can mix it up by using red salsa, jack cheese, or adding drained black beans as well.

| 6-8 PERSON | OVEN | 1 HOUR | $$ |

INGREDIENTS

1 Store Bought Rotisserie Chicken, bones and skin removed and shredded
(Equals About **3 Cups Chicken**)

16 oz Sour Cream

2 ½ cups Cheddar Cheese, shredded
(Reserve About **¼ Cup**)

16 oz Mild Green Tomatillo Salsa

24 Corn Tortillas, torn up

¼ teaspoon Garlic

¼ teaspoon Onion Powder

¼ teaspoon Salt

¼ teaspoon Pepper

DIRECTIONS

STEP 1

In a large bowl, combine sour cream, chicken, cheese and spices. In a casserole dish, layer torn tortillas, chicken mixture and salsa. Repeat and top with remaining cheese.

STEP 2

Cover with foil and bake at 350° for about 35-40 minutes.

CHICKEN SALTIMBOCCA
SUPER FANCY.

MOM TIP

Using a nonstick skillet makes flipping chicken breasts easier, just make sure each side is a nice deep golden brown before flipping it over. You can substitute white wine for the Marsala.

INGREDIENTS

4 Chicken Breasts

4 Slices Prosciutto

12 Leaves Fresh Sage

2 Tablespoons Olive Oil

¼ teaspoon Salt

¼ teaspoon Pepper

3 Tablespoons Marsala

¾ cup Chicken Broth

2 Tablespoons Butter

Toothpicks

4 PERSON **STOVETOP** **30 MINUTES** **$$**

DIRECTIONS

STEP 1

Pound chicken breasts until ½ inch thick. Sprinkle with salt and pepper. Lay 3 fresh sage leaves on each seasoned chicken breast and then top with a slice of prosciutto. Secure with a toothpick. Heat a large frying pan to medium high heat with oil and cook chicken, (prosciutto side down at first) for five minutes without moving chicken. Be careful when turning to keep prosciutto slices and leaves intact. Flip chicken. Cook another five minutes or so until chicken is cooked through.

STEP 2

Remove from pan and keep warm. To the same pan, lower heat to medium and add marsala, scraping pan bottom with a wooden spoon to remove bits. Add chicken broth and simmer until reduced a little. Turn heat off and swirl 2 tablespoons butter into sauce. Serve over chicken breasts. ****PLEASE remove toothpicks before serving, or warn guests****

THE COOKBOOK

CHICKEN POT PIE

A CLASSIC.

MOM TIP

Learn how to make this recipe ASAP because it's a classic! I buy the pre-made crusts in the tin to make life alot easier.

6 PERSON   **OVEN**   **1 HOUR**   **$$**

INGREDIENTS

1 cup Celery, slied

1 cup Onion, diced

1 cup Carrots, sliced

5 Tablespoons All-Purpose Flour

6 Tablespoons Butter

½ cup Chicken Stock

1 cup Half-And-Half

1 teaspoon Salt

½ teaspoon Pepper

2 cups Cooked Diced Chicken

1—10 oz Package Frozen Peas

2 Store Bought Pre-Made Pie Crusts

DIRECTIONS

STEP 1

Melt 1 Tablespoon butter in a medium pot over medium heat. Saute celery, carrots and onion in pot. Saute until tender crisp, just a few minutes. Remove vegetables for the next step. In the same pot over medium heat, melt remaining butter and add the flour and seasonings and cook for one minute. Add chicken stock and half-and-half. Whisk until thickened. Add the sautéed vegetables back to the sauce along with frozen peas and chopped chicken and mix well.

STEP 2

Spoon into one pie crust. Add the other pie crust on top and seal together with the tines of a fork. Poke holes on top for the steam to escape. Bake at 375° for about 50-55 minutes or until the crust is a nice golden brown. Let cool 10 minutes before cutting into wedges.

BBQ CEDAR PLANKED
SALMON

6 PERSON **25 MINUTES** **GRILL**

MOM TIP

Cedar planks are usually sold by the butcher department in a grocery store. Make sure to keep a close eye on the plank as it will get charred and smoke while grilling. Watch it closely and spray any flare ups with water.

DIRECTIONS

STEP 1

Soak the cedar plank in water for about 20 minutes. Spray the top side of the plank with a bit of cooking spray and lay sliced lemons on plank and then the salmon on top of lemons. Season salmon with salt and pepper. In a small bowl, mix the maple syrup and mustard together. Brush on fish. Place plank with fish directly on BBQ and cook for about 15 minutes on medium-high heat, or until fish flakes easily.

INGREDIENTS

1 Whole Salmon Filet

1 Cedar Plank for Grilling

2 Tablespoons Grainy or Dijon Style Mustard

2 teaspoons Maple Syrup

Salt and Pepper

1 Lemon, sliced

  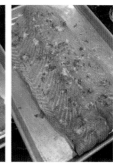

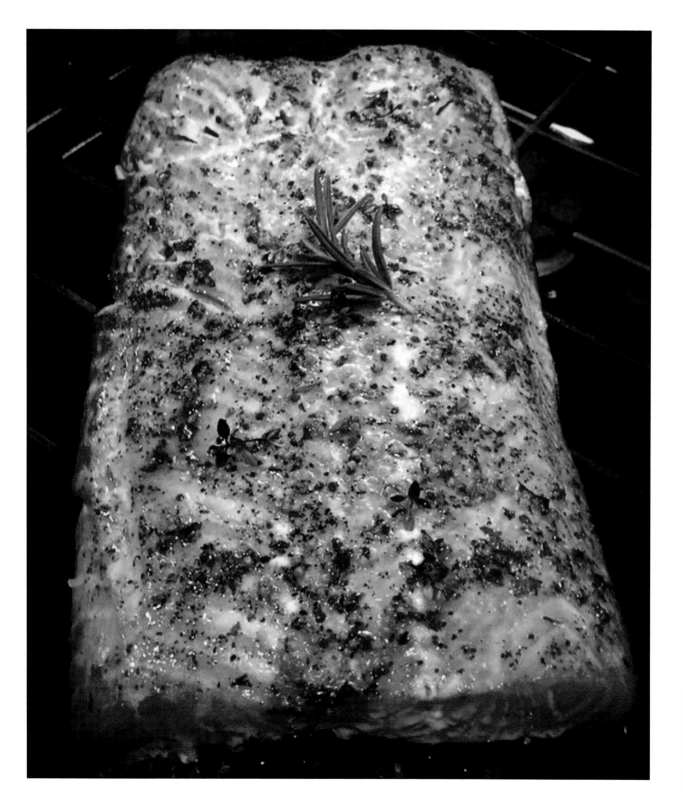

TUNA MELTS
CLASSIC COMFORT.

MOM TIP

This sandwich is impossible to mess up! Don't worry about exact ingredients and feel free to add your own add-ins. If you don't have English muffins, use hamburger buns, French rolls, or toast.

INGREDIENTS

1—7 Oz Can Chunk White Albacore Tuna In Water

1—2 Tablespoons Mayonnaise

1—2 teaspoons Dijon Mustard

2 English Muffins, split

4 Slices Cheddar Cheese

Salt and Pepper

ADD IN'S

2 Tablespoons Diced Celery

2 Tablespoons Diced Carrot

2 teaspoons Minced Onion

2 Tablespoons Lemon Juice

2 Tablespoons Diced Apple

½ teaspoon Dill Weed

Minced Radish

DIRECTIONS

STEP 1

Drain tuna well and add all ingredients to taste. Combine with a fork. Place English muffins on a baking sheet and broil until toasted. Remove from oven and divide tuna onto the muffins. Top with cheese and place back under broiler until cheese is melted.

2-4 PERSON   **TOASTER**   **15 MINUTES**   **$**

KALUA PORK

ON EVERYTHING

MOM TIP

This flavorful roast pork recipe can be used for so many things like tacos, chilequiles, and classic burritos. Mix in some BBQ sauce (pg. 108) and make pulled pork sandwiches. Pork Carnitas are fun to make for a crowd: place a layer of shredded pork on a sheet pan, a few spoonfuls of the broth on top and broil until some bits are crispy. Serve with tortillas, onions, salsa, avocado and cilantro, lime wedges, plus of course rice and beans. Stores and freezes well also! This is a great "bang for your buck" meal – you will have plenty for a crowd or for leftovers.

6 PERSON **CROCKPOT** **6-8 HOURS** **$$$**

INGREDIENTS

3—3½ lb Pork Picnic, Pork Butt Shoulder or Pork Loin

1 whole Banana, upeeled

3 cloves Garlic, whole

1 cup Broth (chicken or vegetable)

2 Tablespoon Liquid Smoke

1 teaspoon Red Salt

1 teaspoon of each > Garlic Powder, Onion Powder, Thyme

*SEE "Sweet & Smoky BBQ Sauce"
(page 107)

DIRECTIONS

STEP 1 •————————

Place pork and liquids in crockpot. Add whole unpeeled banana on top of pork. Season with salt, garlic, onion powder, thyme and liquid smoke. Cover and cook on low for about 6—8 hours or until pork shreds easily. Remove banana and discard.

To shred, remove pork from crockpot. Remove bones (if any) and shred pork with two forks.

(From this point you can use your extra pork for any other recipe).

THE COOKBOOK

CHEESY SCALLOPED POTATOES

EXTREME COMFORT

MOM TIP

This is a must for any family dinner, be sure to alternate layers of potatoes and cheese. You don't need to add ham, but I always do...

6 PERSON   OVEN   60 MINUTES $$

DIRECTIONS

INGREDIENTS •————————————

4 Russet Potatoes, sliced very thin (6 cups)

½ Onion, chopped

¼ cup Butter

¼ cup Flour

Salt and Pepper

2 ½ cups Milk

2 cups Ham, chopped or deli

2 cups Cheddar Cheese, shredded

STEP 1 •————————————

Sauté onions in a bit of butter or olive oil over medium heat, season to taste with salt & pepper. Add the butter and melt. Add the flour and stir for a minute. Add the milk all at once and stir until thickened, then add the ham and cheese. Season with salt & pepper. Layer the potatoes and cheese sauce in a baking dish (Alternating potatoes and cheese sauce) Cover with foil and bake about 40 minutes at 350˚

STEP 2 •————————————

Remove foil and bake another 20 minutes. or until potatoes are fork tender.

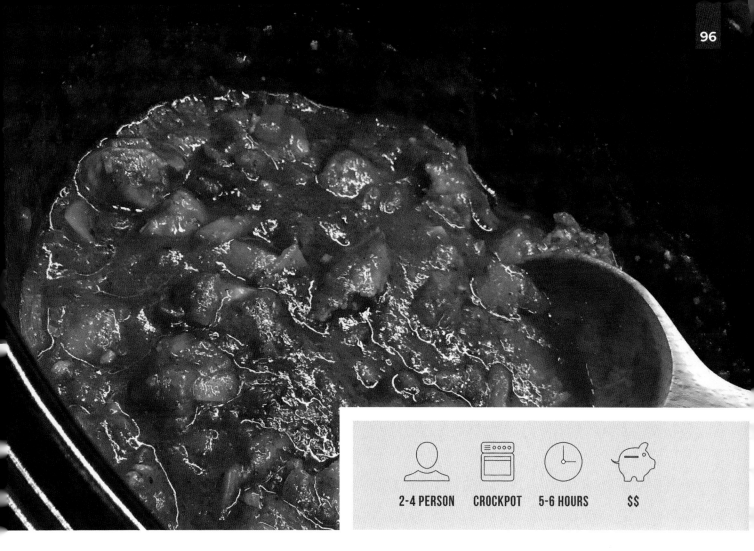

2-4 PERSON **CROCKPOT** **5-6 HOURS** **$$**

ITALIAN SAUSAGE

W/ RED SAUCE

MOM TIP

Add sauce on top of pasta or in a baguette topped with provolone cheese for an easy Italian sandwich.

INGREDIENTS

2 Jars of Good Spaghetti Sauce

1 Package (About 5) Sweet Italian Sausages, casings removed

2 Spicy Italian Sausages, casings removed

1 Onion, diced

½ teaspoon Garlic Powder

1 Package Spaghetti

Parmesan Cheese

DIRECTIONS

STEP 1

Add the spaghetti sauce, sausages, onion, and garlic powder into a crockpot. Turn to low and cook for about 5-6 hours. Cook pasta according to package directions. While pasta is cooking, remove sausages and cut into bite size pieces. Add back to the sauce. and stir. Serve over pasta with parmesan.

BROCCOLI PASTA SAUSAGE

SUPER EASY PREP.

MOM TIP

One of your absolute favorites! Make sure to buy good quality sausages that are fresh. I have used half and half in a pinch with excellent results as well.

6 PERSON   **STOVETOP**   **30 MINUTES**   **$**

COOK LIKE MOM

INGREDIENTS

1 Tablespoon Olive Oil

1 lb Fresh Sweet Italian Sausage, casing removed

2 cups Broccoli Florettes

1 box Penne Pasta

¾ teaspoon Salt

1 cup Heavy Cream

Parmesan Cheese

Salt and Pepper

DIRECTIONS

STEP 1

Boil water in a large pot. Meanwhile, in a large pan over medium high heat, brown sausage, breaking up with the back of a spoon until cooked through. Do not drain. Add half and half plus salt and pepper to taste. Bring to a boil, reduce, and let simmer for about 10 minutes until thickened.

STEP 2

Next add pasta to the boiling water and cook until al dente. Before draining pasta, add broccoli for the last two minutes of cooking. Drain pasta. Add broccoli and pasta to the sausage cream sauce and toss gently. Serve with parmesan cheese.

SNACKS & SAUCES

PASTA PESTO
THE GO TO...

MOM TIP

This can be served over pasta, rice, vegetable. or as a cream sauce over chicken. Just mix pesto with heavy cream over medium high heat in a frying pan until thickened a little. My favorite way to eat pesto is topped on a sliced toasted baguette.

4-6 PERSON

15 MINUTES

$

INGREDIENTS

1 bunch (about **1 ½ - 2 cups**) Fresh Basil Leaves

½ - 1 teaspoon Salt

½ clove Fresh Garlic

½ cup Grated Parmesan Cheese

½ cup Pine Nuts, Walnuts, Pecans, Or Macadamia Nuts

⅓ cup Good Olive Oil

Cooked Pasta

DIRECTIONS

STEP 1

Cook pasta according to directions. Meanwhile, in a food processor or blender, add all of the ingredients and blend until combined. Taste and re-season as needed. Serve over pasta.

GET FANCY.

Popcorn is easy and fast to make. Air poppers are inexpensive and the most simple way to make popcorn. Just start sprinkling, mixing, and tasting with these recipes. You'll come up with some winners on your own!

INGREDIENTS: 3 TABLESPOONS OF BUTTER, 8 CUPS OF POPCORN

Seasonings depending on recipe:
italian seasonings, onion powder, garlic powder, shredded parmesan cheese, chili powder, dried parsley flakes, ranch seasoning packet, sugar, cinnamon, salt and pepper...

POPCORN

TECHNIQUES

ITALIAN:

Melt about 3 tablespoons of butter. Drizzle over popcorn and toss to coat. In a little bowl, add about a teaspoon of italian seasonings and ⅛ teaspoon onion and garlic powder. Drizzle over popcorn and toss to coat. Season popcorn with salt to taste and add shredded parmesan cheese. Toss.

SPICY CHILI:

Melt about 3 Tablespoons of butter. Drizzle over popcorn and toss to coat. In a little bowl, mix about ¼ teaspoon chili powder, ⅛ teaspoon pepper and 1 teaspoon dried parsley flakes. Pour over buttered popcorn and toss. Season popcorn with salt to taste and add shredded parmesan cheese. Toss.

RANCH:

Melt about 3 tablespoons of butter. Drizzle over popcorn and toss to coat. Sprinkle with 1-2 teaspoons of a ranch seasoning packet and toss to coat.

SALTY SWEET:

Melt about 3 tablespoons of butter. Drizzle over popcorn and toss to coat. In a little bowl, mix about 1 tablespoon sugar and ¼ teaspoon cinnamon, ¼ teaspoon salt. Pour over popcorn and toss to coat.

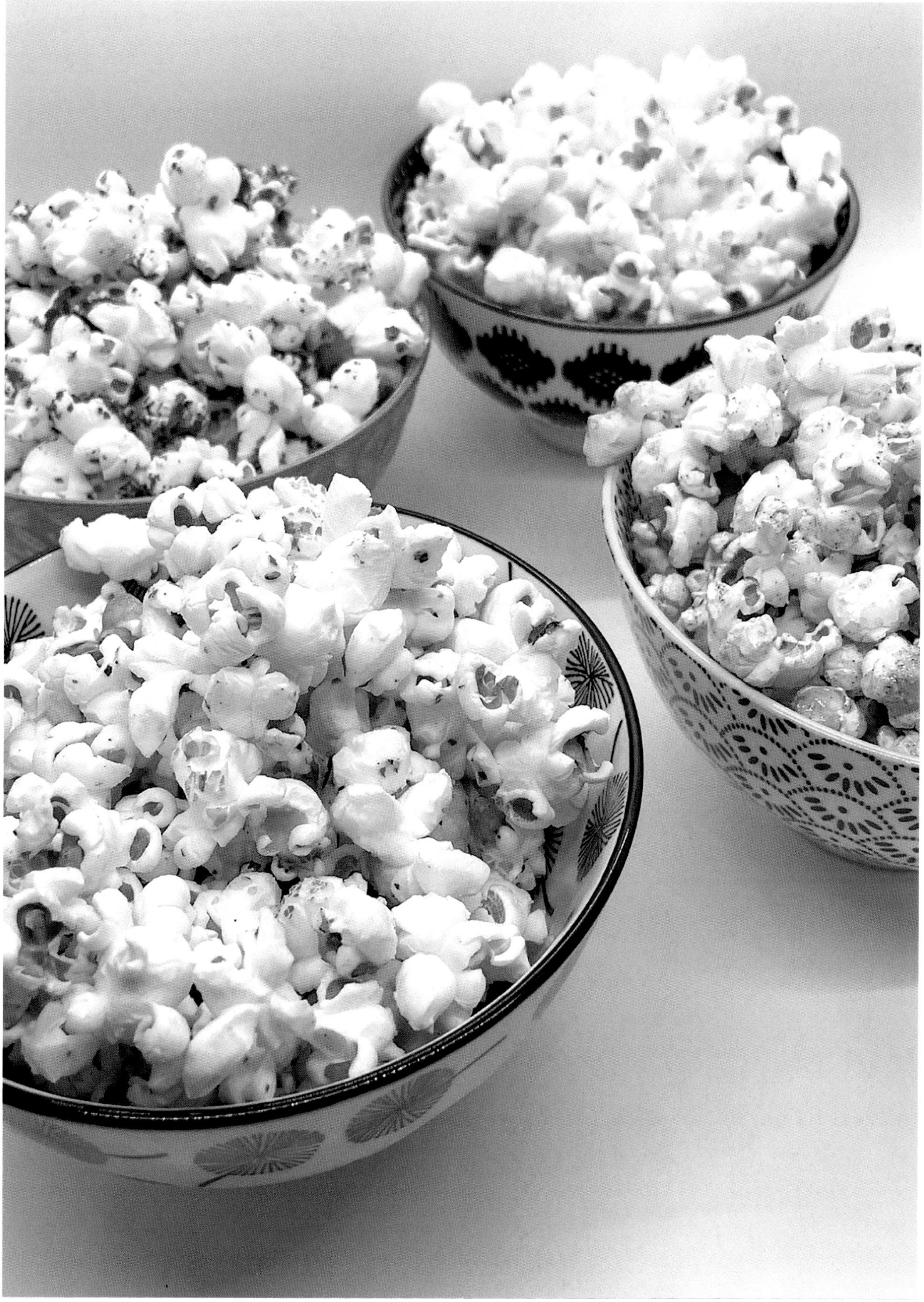

RESTAURANT SALSA
& PICO DE GALLO

MOM TIP

You'll most likely have everything in your pantry to make one or the other.

2 CUPS   **10 MINUTES**   **$**

DIRECTIONS

STEP 1

Mix all together to taste. Serve with tortilla chips.

PICO DE GALLO INGREDIENTS

½ cup Sweet Onion, minced

1 cup Chopped Tomatoes

1 cup Cilantro, chopped

1-2 Seeded and Diced Jalapeños To Taste

Salt and Pepper

Juice of a Lime

COOK LIKE MOM

SALSA INGREDIENTS

1-4 oz can Chopped Green Chilies

1 Bunch Green Onions, diced

1 Bunch Cilantro, minced

1-12 ounce Can Whole Tomatoes Chopped Up And Juice Reserved

Garlic Powder

Salt and Pepper

DIRECTIONS

STEP 1

Mix all together to taste. Serve with tortilla chips.

CHIMICHURRI
SAUCE

MOM TIP

Chop and mix this by hand, don't use a blender. Start with the minimum amounts and add more to your taste. We love to serve this over grilled tri tip or flank steak. I like it over white rice too! For a party appetizer try grilling a tri tip or steak and slicing into bit sized pieces. Serve with chimmichurri on the side and toothpicks!

INGREDIENTS

1 bunch (about 1-1 ½ cups)
   Flat Leaf Parsley, finely chopped

¼ cup Red Onion, minced

2 Tablespoons Dried Oregano

½ - ¾ cup Olive Oil

2—3 Tablespoons Red Wine Vinegar

½ teaspoon Salt

¼ teaspoon Pepper

½ teaspoon Red Chili Flakes

DIRECTIONS

STEP 1

Gently mix together all ingredients. Taste and re-season if needed.

4 PERSON

15 MINUTES

$

SWEET & SMOKY
BBQ SAUCE

MOM TIP

This BBQ sauce is so easy to put together... don't be intimidated by the list of ingredients. Great over ribs, pulled pork or sliced brisket.

COOK LIKE MOM

INGREDIENTS

14 oz Catsup

3 Tablespoons Liquid Smoke

3 Tablespoons Worcestershire Sauce

3 Tablespoons Brown Sugar

3 Tablespoons Chili Powder

1 Tablespoon Mustard

1 teaspoon Celery Seed

¼ teaspoon Cayenne Pepper

½ teaspoon Salt

½ teaspoon Pepper

4 Tablespoons Butter

DIRECTIONS

STEP 1

Add all ingredients in a small pot and simmer for about 5 minutes.

2 CUPS **10 MINUTES** **$**

MONSTER COOKIES
WHAT A TREAT.

MOM TIP

Use parchment paper when making any cookies! They will remove from the cookie sheet so much easier.

INGREDIENTS

3 Eggs

1 cup Sugar

1 cup Brown Sugar

1 Tablespoon Vanilla

2 teaspoons Baking Soda

1 stick Butter, softened

1 ½ cups Peanut Butter

4 ½ cups Oats

1 cup Chocolate Chips

1 cup Plain Chocolate Coated Candy Pieces

2 1/2 DOZEN   **OVEN**   **30 MINUTES**   **$$**

DIRECTIONS

STEP 1

Preheat oven to 350°. Using an electric mixer, mix all ingredients until combined. Drop onto a cookie sheet about golf ball size. (You can use an ice cream scoop).

STEP 2

Bake for about 13-15 minutes depending on your oven or until golden brown. Let cool a few minutes before removing from the cookie sheet.

FRANGIPANE TART

AN EASY DESSERT.

MOM TIP

Buying a pre-made pie crust is a quick version to making this tart and It always turns out beautifully.

6 PIECES   **OVEN**   **45 MINUTES**   **$**

INGREDIENTS ●————————

1½ sticks Butter, softened

1½ cups White Sugar

3 Eggs, beaten

1½ cups Ground Almonds (Almond Flour)

¼ cup All-Purpose Flour

1 teaspoon Vanilla

3 Tablespoons, Any Jam or Jelly

1 pie crust, Thawed if Frozen, prepared in a pan

DIRECTIONS

STEP 1 ●————————

Pierce holes with a fork to the bottom of the pie crust. Partially bake pie crust for about 10 minutes at 375°. While that bakes mix the butter, sugar, eggs, almond flour, flour, and vanilla. Once the pie shell is partially cooled, spread the jam on the bottom of the pie crust. Then top with the almond filling. Bake at 375° for about 25-30 minutes or until the middle is just set and the crust is golden.

PAVLOVA

AN AUSSIE TREAT.

MOM TIP:

This is my favorite dessert to make! It's important to make this on a nice day, not a humid or rainy day since the shell won't dry out. Sometimes, I add just a bit of lemon curd on top of cooked and cooled pavlova, before adding adding the whipped cream and berries.

4-6 PERSON **OVEN** **1.5HOURS** **$**

INGREDIENTS

4 Egg Whites

1 teaspoon Vanilla Extract

1 teaspoon Fresh Lemon Juice or White Vinegar

2 teaspoons Cornstarch

1 pint Heavy Cream, whipped

1 cup Various Berries
1 cup White Sugar

DIRECTIONS

STEP 1

Preheat oven to 300°. Line a baking pan with parchment paper. With an electric mixer, beat egg whites until just stiff. Slowly add the sugar while beating. Continue to beat until egg whites are glossy. Stop beating and sprinkle on cornstarch, lemon juice and vanilla. Fold in. Spoon the mixture into an 8 or 9 inch circle, making a nest shape with the middle being a little thinner than the sides. Bake for about 1 hour. Remove and cool. Top with whipped cream first, then berries.

GINA HAS BEEN A PERSONAL CHEF FOR 17+ YEARS. SHE LOVES TO INVITE HER FRIENDS AND FAMILY INTO THE KITCHEN TO SHARE IN HER PASSION AND CREATE A GREAT MEAL TOGETHER...